Major alterations and conversions:
a BRE guide to radon remedial measures in existing dwellings

C R Scivyer, MCIOB

Building Research Establishment
Garston
Watford
WD2 7JR

Prices for all available
BRE publications can be
obtained from:
BRE Bookshop
Building Research Establishment
Garston, Watford, WD2 7JR
Telephone: 0923 664444

BR 267
ISBN 0 85125 638 4

CONTENTS

INTRODUCTION

This report is one of a series giving practical advice on methods of reducing radon levels in existing dwellings. It deals specifically with dwellings, and supplements the general guidance given in *The householders' guide to radon*[1], obtainable from local environmental health officers or from the Department of the Environment.

This report offers advice on radon-protective measures that can be taken during the planning and implementation of major alteration or conversion works to a building in radon-affected areas. It describes how certain precautionary measures can help to reduce indoor radon levels, and can make it easier to resolve any future radon problem. This is particularly relevant when converting redundant farm or other out-buildings into living accommodation, or carrying out major works such as floor replacement in older properties.

BACKGROUND TO RADON
What is radon?

Radon is a colourless, odourless, radioactive gas. It comes from the radioactive decay of uranium. Uranium acts as a permanent source of radon and is found in small quantities in all soils and rocks, although the amount varies from place to place. It is particularly prevalent in granite areas. Radon levels vary not only between different parts of the country but even between neighbouring buildings.

Radon in the soil and rocks mixes with air and rises to the surface where it is quickly diluted in the atmosphere. Concentrations in the open air are low. Radon that enters enclosed spaces, such as dwellings, can reach relatively high concentrations.

The floors and walls of dwellings contain a multiplicity of small cracks and holes (Figure 1) formed during and after construction. The air pressure inside the building is slightly lower than that outside, because of the heating of the dwelling and the effect of the wind. The fact that the air pressure in the soil is higher than that in the dwelling causes radon-laden air to flow through cracks and holes in the ground into the dwelling.

Measuring radon

Before carrying out any major alteration or conversion works to a building it is important to establish whether it would be appropriate to incorporate radon-protective measures within the building. The local authority's environmental health officer will be able to tell you whether the building is in an area with high radon levels. Once this has been established, if it is occupied, the building should be monitored to find out whether it has a radon problem.

Experience has shown that radon concentrations in adjacent buildings, even adjoining ones, can differ by as much as ten times, so measurement results from neighbouring properties are not reliable indicators. The average radon level of the district as a whole is a

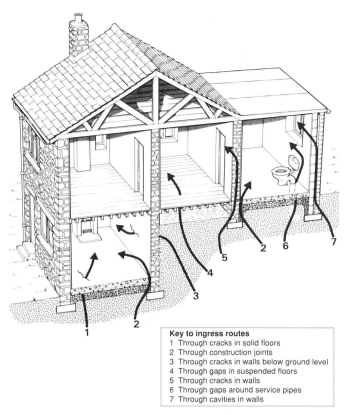

Key to ingress routes
1 Through cracks in solid floors
2 Through construction joints
3 Through cracks in walls below ground level
4 Through gaps in suspended floors
5 Through cracks in walls
6 Through gaps around service pipes
7 Through cavities in walls

Figure 1 Routes by which radon enters a dwelling

good indicator, however. The Department of the Environment suggests an action level of 200 Bq/m^3 for dwellings, and recommends that remedial measures be taken where levels are higher than this. If the building is found to have a high radon level then measures can be incorporated within the alteration works to reduce the level. It will not be possible to monitor an unoccupied building, such as a derelict farm building, so preventative measures should be installed as a precaution.

For further information on radon and radon monitoring, contact the National Radiological Protection Board, Chilton, Didcot, Oxon, OX11 0RQ.

ALTERATION AND CONVERSION WORK

Once the extent of the radon problem has been established, appropriate measures can be considered for inclusion within the alteration or conversion work. Alteration work can involve the replacement of floors or windows, or the addition of a new bathroom, kitchen or heating system. In cases where houses are being converted into flats, the concern will lie with those rooms with floors or walls in direct contact with the ground. In each case, radon-protective measures should be considered. Guidance on surveying dwellings with high indoor radon levels is available in a BRE Report[2].

Replacement floors

Replacing the floor is one of the most disruptive alterations that can be made to a building and can have the greatest impact on indoor radon levels. Often a new in-situ concrete floor is installed to replace a poor-quality concrete or suspended timber floor. It might be assumed that replacing the floor with a new one will solve the radon problem. In most cases, a new concrete floor incorporating a damp-proof membrane is likely to lead to some improvement. However, there will still be a very small gap wherever the floor meets the wall caused by slight shrinkage of concrete when it cures. Radon can enter through this gap.

Radon can also enter around service entry points. These cannot always be sealed; in some cases a seal proves inadequate or the membrane simply diverts the radon to enter the living space elsewhere, perhaps through the walls. Additional precautionary measures, such as provision for subfloor depressurisation (sump system) should therefore be considered when replacing the floor.

While it is advisable to provide for future subfloor depressurisation, it is still important to design the floor to minimise radon entry. The damp-proof membrane is an important part of the floor since it will double as a radon barrier if all joints in the damp-proof membrane are sealed. A membrane of 300 micrometre (1200 gauge) polyethylene (Polythene) sheet will generally be adequate. (Some diffusion will occur through the sheet but this diffusion can be ignored as most radon entry is through cracks.) Reinforced polyethylene sheet should be considered where there is a risk of puncturing the membrane.

The membrane can be constructed using other materials which match the airtightness and water-proofing properties offered by polyethylene. Suitable alternative materials include modern flexible sheet roofing materials, pre-fabricated welded barriers, liquid coatings, self-adhesive bituminous-coated sheet products, and asphalt. All are likely to prove more expensive than polyethylene sheet, however.

Where possible, service entries should not penetrate the radon-proof membrane. Where this is not possible, an airtight seal should be constructed around each entry. Prefabricated 'top hat' sections are available from some membrane manufacturers for sealing around pipe entries (Figure 2).

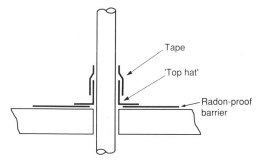

Figure 2 Achieving an airtight seal around service penetrations

Although it is difficult to ensure a complete seal, it is worth trying to seal the gap at the edge of the new floor. This might be achieved in one of three ways:

- By sealing the damp-proof membrane to the wall with a mastic or adhesive before pouring the concrete slab.
- By trying to seal the gap after the slab has cured.
- Where there is a damp-proof course within the wall, by sealing it to the damp/radon-proof barrier in the floor.

Sealing the gap on completion is probably the easiest option, although it will be necessary to leave the slab to cure for several weeks before applying the sealant. Consider also the sealant's life expectancy, as replacement later may prove difficult. Even when the edge is sealed it may still be necessary to provide subfloor depressurisation.

It is also important to prevent damp ingress as well as radon entry when replacing a floor. A BRE leaflet gives additional guidance on preventing moisture entry[3].

An old timber floor should not usually be completely replaced with a new timber floor, although simple repairs to an existing timber floor would obviously be acceptable. If the complete floor requires replacement, it is preferable to install an in-situ concrete floor with provision for sub-slab depressurisation.

Existing floors
It would seem sensible to try to seal all obvious cracks, gaps and holes in the floors to prevent radon from entering the building. Sealing a large hole can produce a dramatic reduction in the radon level. However, in practice it has been found that the reduction is not always as large as had been hoped for. Sealing solid floors has produced reductions of a half to two-thirds on average. The reasons for this are not entirely clear, but probably have something to do with the fact that it is difficult to ensure that all the cracks have been found, or the resistance to flow is in the soil. It is difficult, for example, to seal floor edge gaps without removing skirting boards.

In particular, cracks and joints behind kitchen units, built-in cupboards and boxed pipework can easily be neglected, perhaps because they are difficult to get at, and yet they may provide major flow paths for radon. It is also difficult to get at cracks and joints under staircases. To gain access you have to move cupboards fixed to the floor, and this may be disruptive and costly. Trying to seal cracks by removing cupboard plinths and working through the low openings will rarely be successful. Boxed pipework should be opened at ground level so that you can make a proper assessment of the sealing requirements.

Although other solutions may be more appropriate, it is still worthwhile sealing all the major leakage paths. With suspended concrete floors this is likely to involve only the sealing of gaps around service entry or exit points. With suspended timber floors, it again means sealing gaps around service entry or exit points, but also, possibly, major joints between floorboards. With suspended timber floors, sealing must be accompanied by proper ventilation of the underfloor space. Sealing of the bulk floor area using impervious sheet materials such as polyethylene is not recommended because of the risk of causing rot in the timber.

In spite of the disappointing results reported, sealing remains an attractive remedial treatment for radon levels up to 400 or 500 Bq/m^3. Sealing can be cheap in terms of materials, may not cause too much disruption, and is passive; in other words it costs nothing to run. Tracing and sealing all the cracks can be time consuming, but it is an attractive option for house owners carrying out their own remedial measures as the material costs are low. If a builder is employed it will be more expensive.

Further guidance can be found in a BRE Report on sealing floors[4].

Subfloor depressurisation

It is advisable when installing an in-situ concrete floor to provide a radon sump beneath the slab. This will enable subfloor depressurisation to be introduced relatively easily if required at a later date. Subfloor depressurisation involves sucking radon-laden air from beneath a building and discharging it harmlessly into the atmosphere (see Figure 3).

A single sump will probably be sufficient for a typical house. Where clean permeable fill has been used, a single sump is likely to have an influence over an area of approximately 250 m^2, or for a distance of 15 m from the sump. Ideally this should be positioned centrally under the house so that its pipe entry is not blocked when the fill is placed. Fill used beneath the slab

should not contain excessive fines, to allow for maximum depressurisation.

A simple sump (often referred to as a standard sump) can be constructed using bricks laid loose in a honeycomb bond so as to form a box around the end of the pipe (Figures 4 and 5). Prefabricated sump units are also available from some builders merchants. The pipe should typically be 110 mm diameter uPVC with joints using standard couplings sealed and airtight. The pipe can either be routed up through the building to exit through the roof or taken out through an external wall. If the building is known to have a radon problem, a fan can be connected to the pipework during construction, and can be activated on completion. If it is not known whether the building has a radon problem, the pipework can simply be capped off until the completed building has been monitored for radon.

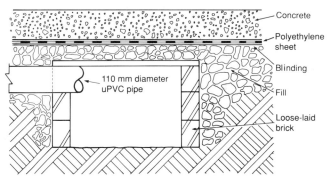

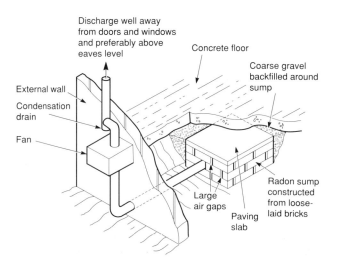

Figure 4 Radon sump details

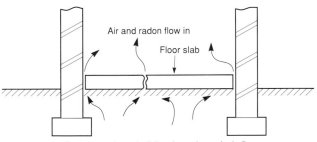

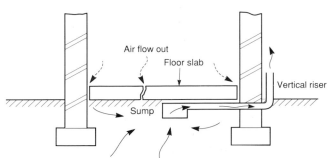

Figure 3 The effect of a radon sump

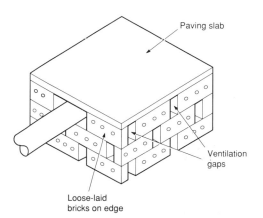

Figure 5 Construction of a standard radon sump

3

Where new concrete floors are not being installed, subfloor depressurisation should still be considered. In such cases mini-sump (Figure 6) or externally excavated systems (Figure 7) may be appropriate. In both cases the sump is constructed by scooping out about a bucketful of fill from beneath the floor slab. Installing one of these systems whilst carrying out other works is likely to be less expensive in the long term, less disruptive and easier to disguise as part of the other works.

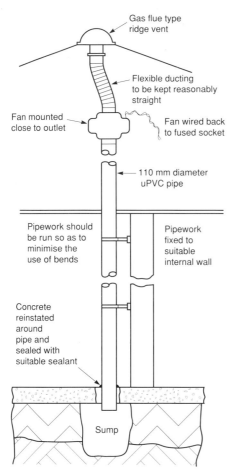

Figure 6 The internal sump with internal pipework

If a fan is installed, it should be positioned with the outlet well away from windows, doors and ventilation grilles, ideally discharging just above eaves level.

Subfloor depressurisation is usually achieved actively using an electric fan to provide suction. In some cases it is possible to use the suction effects of the wind over the pipe outlet and natural stack effect in the pipework to operate the sump system passively. A passive stack subfloor depressurisation system comprises a vertical stack pipe run from the radon sump vertically through the house to discharge at a point just above eaves or at ridge level. However, passive sump systems are less successful than those fitted with fans. They are probably only appropriate for lower levels of radon. A passive system which fails to work can be easily upgraded later by installing a fan.

To avoid penetrating the radon-proof membrane in the floor unnecessarily the pipe can be taken through the

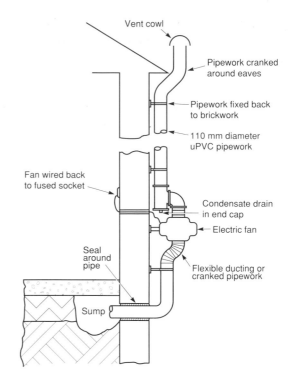

Figure 7 The externally excavated sump

wall, not up through the floor. However, it may be desired for aesthetic reasons to locate pipework in ducts inside the house and to take the outlet from the fan through the roof. It is **not satisfactory** for the fan to ventilate into a roof space. If a fan is fitted it should always be placed as close to the outlet as possible in order to keep the pipework always under suction. This is particularly important when routing pipework inside the house as even slight leaks could increase indoor radon levels.

If the subfloor area comprises several compartments, sumps may be required for each compartment. These may be connected to a manifold and a single fan although there is usually no need to establish a manifold of pipes since a single sump will suffice if placed along the separating wall, with a few bricks omitted to allow depressurisation (Figure 8). It is important for fill beneath the slab to contain minimal fines so as not to impair the efficiency of the depressurisation system.

If the alteration work includes replacing an underfloor ducted warm air heating system with another form of heating, it might be possible to use the redundant

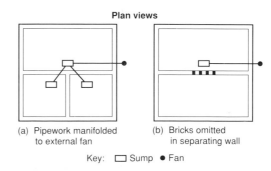

Figure 8 Location of sumps within multi-compartment subfloor areas

underfloor ducting as a large sump. This can be achieved by sealing up the ventilation grilles and connecting the ductwork to a fan (Figure 9).

Fans and pipework should be located where noise disturbance will be minimal. All fans create noise and vibration. Clearly the louder the noise and greater the vibration caused by the fan, and the closer the source of noise to the listener, the greater the potential

Floor and wall grilles

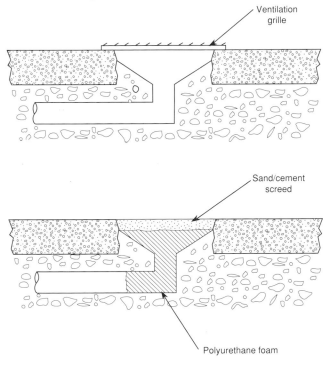

Heater unit plenum and ducts

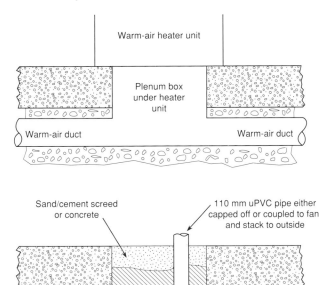

Figure 9 How to convert a redundant ducted warm-air heating system into a sump system

problem will be. Selection of a quieter fan can help, but its location is more important.

Systems, especially the fans, should be positioned as far as possible from any noise-sensitive area, and mounted on a part of the structure which does not respond to vibration. Ideally, the fan should be fixed to a heavy structure such as a concrete, blockwork or brickwork wall. Soft or flexible fixing to a roof truss, beam or rafter may also be appropriate. Avoid fixing to a light-weight internal partition or ceiling. Design the system to avoid bends unless they are strictly necessary. Noise transmission can be reduced further by using flexible couplings between the fan and ductwork, and by supporting the fan on non-rigid mounts. Further information on minimising noise can be found in a BRE leaflet[5].

Pipework to sump systems should be self-draining, to avoid condensation damage to fans and noise from bubbling condensate trapped in U-bends. Keep fans close to outlets to reduce condensation and ensure that the maximum length of pipework is under suction, minimising the risk of re-entrainment.

Note the risk in some extreme cases, where houses are very airtight and have open-flued appliances or open fires, that a sump could draw flue gases back into the house. It is obviously vital that this should not happen. Further research is being carried out in this area. In the interim, BRE recommends that you avoid locating a sump beneath a room with an open-flued appliance or an open fire. Further advice is available in a BRE leaflet[6], or telephone the BRE Radon Hotline (0923 664707). You should also ensure that you do not install an oversized sump fan.

A BRE Report[7] offers more comprehensive guidance on the installation of radon sumps.

Underfloor ventilation

Whilst carrying out other works to the house it is important to ensure that suspended ground floors are adequately ventilated. With a suspended timber floor, improved ventilation will not only reduce the indoor radon level, it will also help to reduce the risk of timber rotting.

Where the radon level is only just above the recommended action level, say 200–300 Bq/m^3, a reduction to below the action level might be achieved by clearing obstructions from existing vents. For higher radon levels or where there are not enough vents, the installation of additional vents would be appropriate. This can be done through the external walls, just below the floor.

Where vents are provided through cavity walls they should be sleeved. This is of particular importance where the cavity wall has been or is going to be insulated.

5

Ideally, the openings should be provided on at least two opposite walls, and should be large enough to give an actual opening of at least 1500 mm^2 for each metre run of wall. Plastic louvred ventilators are preferable to clay airbricks, as they usually offer greater open area and fewer of them will be needed (Figure 10). Replacing terracotta airbricks with the same overall size of plastic louvred airbrick is a convenient way of improving the ventilation under a floor without the need to break-out many new airbrick openings. Do not leave vents without some form of vermin guard.

If a concrete floor is to replace a suspended timber floor, it is important to ensure that underfloor ventilation of adjacent timber floors is not impaired, so as to reduce the risk of timber rot. This might be achieved either by increasing the number of vents elsewhere or by ducting air under the new floor (Figure 11).

Vents should not be cut into suspended timber floors; ventilation should always be provided beneath the floor.

If natural ventilation proves inadequate in reducing the indoor radon level, then you may have to install an electric fan to increase the airflow under the floor. Fans can be installed to suck or blow. Where a fan is used to suck air from the sub-floor void the operation of open-flued combustion appliances may be affected. In that case blowing may be more satisfactory.

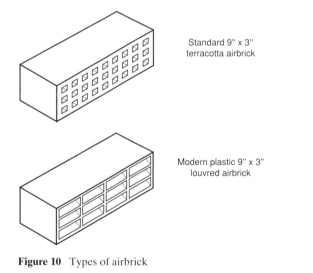

Standard 9" x 3" terracotta airbrick

Modern plastic 9" x 3" louvred airbrick

Figure 10 Types of airbrick

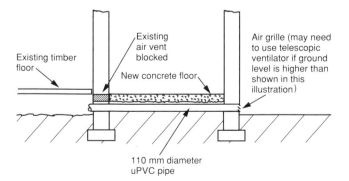

Existing timber floor

Existing air vent blocked

New concrete floor

Air grille (may need to use telescopic ventilator if ground level is higher than shown in this illustration)

110 mm diameter uPVC pipe

Figure 11 Maintaining subfloor ventilation using ducts beneath new concrete floor

Experience with blowing is limited, but in some cases it may prove more effective than suction. There could be problems of draughts inside the house with the system blowing. On the other hand, suction applied by an oversized fan could draw warm moist air from the house down into the underfloor space, bringing potential timber rot problems.

When considering increasing the air movement under the floor, you should check whether services routed under the floor, particularly central heating or water pipes, could be put at risk from freezing. It may be necessary to insulate vulnerable pipework.

Replacement windows
If the windows are to be replaced as part of the alteration or conversion works it is worth considering windows fitted with trickle vents.

Ventilation
While improvements to the way in which a house is ventilated can help to reduce indoor radon levels (Figure 12), increased ventilation can affect indoor comfort, so this may not be the best solution.

Recommended actions include installing trickle ventilators, capping chimneys and avoiding open fires, but these are still likely to have only a modest effect on indoor radon levels. They should be contemplated on their own only in houses which have radon levels close to the action level.

If trickle ventilators are to be installed in existing windows as a radon remedial measure, they must be located downstairs rather than upstairs. They should be permanently open, to sustain the reduction in radon. Ideally they should not be too large, with a typical surface area of 4000 mm^2 to 6000 mm^2 in each room. They are usually located at the tops of windows to reduce draughts.

Any unused chimneys should be blocked up, as they tend to draw air out of the room and reduce pressure in the room, thus drawing in radon. If you decide to block them up permanently, you should also take action to prevent condensation building up inside the chimney. Cap the chimney stack with a chimney-pot hood and provide a small ventilation opening of about 50 mm × 20 mm in the blocked-up fireplace. A BRE leaflet[8] deals with this in greater detail.

If the house has a gas-, coal- or oil-fired appliance that discharges into a chimney (ie an open-flued appliance) replace it with a balanced-flue appliance or ensure that there is an adequate supply of fresh air into the room from outside the house. Open coal or wood fires and open solid-fuel-effect gas fires in particular can draw large volumes of air out of a room, even when they are provided with an underfloor supply of air directly to the fire. If an alternative form of heating is available, and the householder can do without an open fire, then it is worth considering blocking up the chimney as just

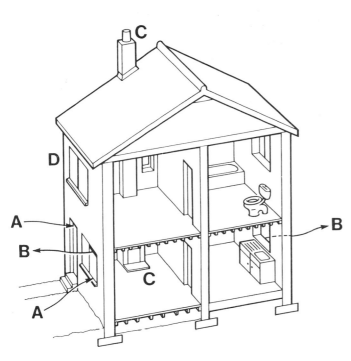

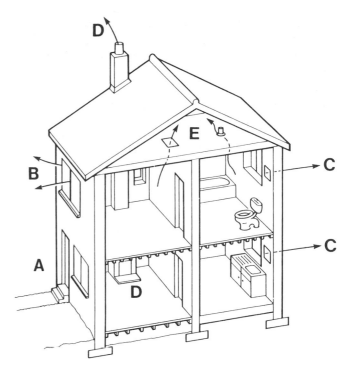

Good ventilation practice will help to limit radon entry
A   Leave some cracks around doors and windows, use ground-floor windows for ventilation
B   Fit trickle ventilators in ground-floor windows
C   Cap-off and seal up unused chimneys
D   Seal cracks around first-floor windows

Poor ventilation practice will increase radon entry
A   Ground-floor windows sealed
B   First-floor windows unsealed
C   Extract fans used for long periods
D   Use of open fires especially with unrestricted chimneys, unused chimneys left open
E   Poor sealing around traps and pipes in roof

Figure 12 Good and poor ventilation practice

described. Closed appliances such as 'room heaters' and 'stoves' (generally these are appliances consisting of a box with a door, which is normally closed, connected to the chimney by a flue pipe) are preferred to open fires and open solid-fuel-effect gas appliances.

Most modern central heating boilers and some gas fires will have balanced flues. These take all the air they need for combustion and get rid of all the exhaust gases through the same metal terminal in the wall. As they draw no air from the house, they are ideal for radon-affected areas. If you plan to install or renew the central heating boiler, a balanced-flue room-sealed type without an underfloor draught is preferable. This may mean that you have to move the boiler to a suitable external wall, although fan-assisted balanced-flue appliances are available and they overcome this problem.

Ensure that kitchen and bathroom extract fans are appropriately sized. An appropriate axial or propeller-type fan for a typical house should have an impeller no greater than 150 mm in diameter. Extract fans should not need to be run continuously.

It is not uncommon to find vents cut into suspended timber floors, either to provide ventilation to a combustion appliance or to increase ventilation of the underfloor space. These vents can act as major entry routes for radon. They should therefore be sealed up and alternative ventilation provided above or below the floor.

Basements and cellars
Basements and cellars are relatively uncommon in the UK but are likely to be major contributors to the radon problem. The type of solution that can be applied to houses with basements will be determined by several factors: the size and location of the basement, to what extent it is utilised, the type of construction of the basement walls and floor, the type of construction of the ground floor and, to a certain extent, the radon level.

The most obvious solution may appear to be to seal up cracks and gaps in the basement walls and floor. It is worth trying to seal major gaps, but to do more may prove both difficult and expensive. If the basement is being renovated for frequent use, then it may be worthwhile tanking it. Tanking, which involves coating the walls and floor with a waterproof barrier, is likely to be expensive. It could, however, prevent problems of dampness as well as reducing the radon level in the basement. Unfortunately, in cases where the basement is beneath only part of the house, sealing the basement alone may solve only part of the problem.

With moderate levels of radon, increased natural ventilation may be the appropriate solution. If the basement is unheated and little used, then this may be done by installing air vents, or increasing the size and number of existing vents. With higher radon levels it may be necessary to fit a fan to increase the air movement. Reduction in levels of up to 10:1 have been achieved. If the basement is to be occupied then increased ventilation may not be acceptable. In such cases, an active solution such as a sump system or positive pressurisation may have to be used, even though the radon level is low.

With high levels of radon it is likely that a sump system will be required. The number and location of sumps will depend on the house. It will probably be easier to install such a system in the basement than elsewhere, although in many cases this will involve installing a new concrete floor. If the basement extends under only part of the house, the system installed there is likely to influence the radon level in only that part of the house. However, if the adjacent ground floor is of solid concrete, the sump system in the basement could be manifolded to deal with this additional part of the house (Figure 13). If the adjacent ground floor is of suspended timber construction, it may be necessary to deal with the timber floor separately.

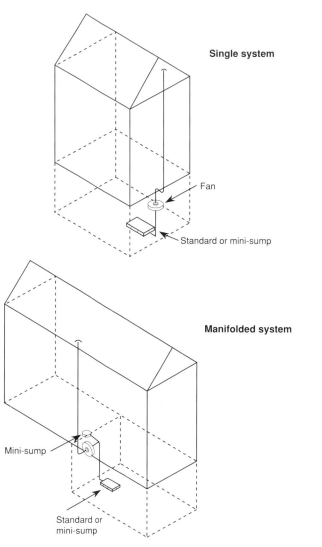

Figure 13 Single and multi-sump systems for use in basements

BATHROOM, KITCHEN OR OTHER EXTENSIONS: ADDITIONAL POINTS TO CONSIDER
Underfloor vents
If the existing house has suspended ground floors it is important to ensure that the extension does not impair the underfloor ventilation. This is particularly important with suspended timber floors where adequate ventilation is necessary to reduce the risk of timber rot. It has been common practice for existing underfloor vents either to be permanently blocked or left so they open directly into the extension. As far as radon is concerned, the vents should either be permanently blocked up and an alternative supply of air provided to the underfloor space, or opened up (where the vents are low enough) and air ducted under the new floor of the extension (Figure 14).

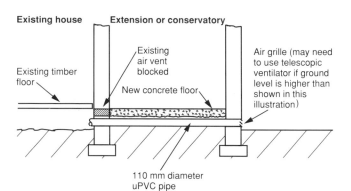

Figure 14 Maintaining subfloor ventilation using ducts under floor of extension

Suspended timber floors
The use of suspended timber floors in radon-affected areas is inadvisable. It has been found that high indoor radon levels are common, even where a suspended timber floor has good ventilation and the soil below is covered with a polyethylene damp-proof barrier and concrete covering.

Service penetrations
Avoid routing services through the floor, if possible. If this cannot be avoided, try to seal around each penetration by sealing the service pipe to the radon-proof or damp-proof barrier using a suitable adhesive tape or proprietary sealing collar. Alternatively, seal once the floor is installed. Where large gaps occur, fill with sand–cement mortar; for small gaps, seal with a bathroom sealant or mastic. A BRE Report[4] offers further guidance on sealing.

Construction joints
The construction joint between the new floor and the existing dwelling should be sealed, if possible. Where both the new and existing floors incorporate a radon-proof barrier, the two should be jointed where they meet within the wall. It will prove difficult not to damage the existing barrier when trying to break out sufficient mortar to allow access for sealing. The alternative might be to cut a chase slightly above or

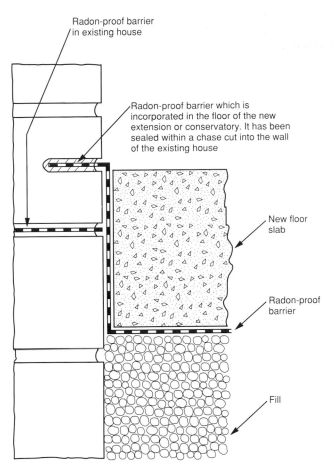

Figure 15 Method of jointing radon-proof barrier in new floor to existing dpc or radon-proof barrier

below the barrier in the wall, into which the new barrier can be tucked. If the existing floor does not incorporate a radon-proof barrier, seal the joint between the new floor and wall using a bathroom sealant or other flexible filler (Figure 15).

Reducing the radon level in the whole house

You should consider incorporating radon-reduction measures within the extension that could be used for the whole house, regardless of whether the house has been monitored for radon. The following approaches should be considered:

- If the main part of the house has a solid concrete floor, and the extension is to have a solid concrete floor, install a radon sump during the construction of the extension.

- If the main part of the house is known to have a high radon level, install and activate a complete sump system.

- If the house has yet to be monitored, install just the sump and pipework. The system could then be activated at a later date, if necessary.

The most appropriate location for the sump is along the wall of the main house. Its effect on the main house is maximised if it is connected through the wall to the fill beneath the house (Figures 16 and 17).

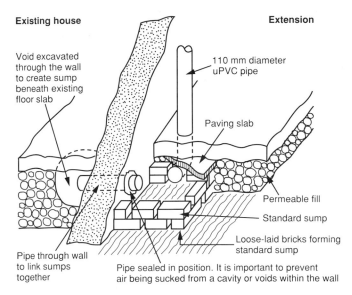

Figure 16 Details of radon sump system in extension

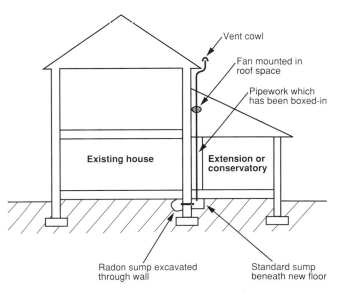

Figure 17 Layout of radon sump system in extension

Building Regulations requirements for extensions

In certain areas radon-protective measures for extensions may be necessary to comply with the Building Regulations. You should contact your Local Authority Building Control Department to find out whether protective measures are necessary in your area. Requirement C2 of Schedule 1 of the Building Regulations 1991 for England and Wales refers to the BRE Report *Radon: guidance on protective measures for new dwellings*[9] which gives the following advice:

*It is advisable when a house is extended that radon-protective measures be incorporated in the new work. For **a house with radon-protective measures** the extension should include protective measures equivalent to those in the existing house. Consideration should be given to linking the radon-proof barrier in the new floor to the radon-proof barrier in the existing house.*

*Within the [defined] areas, an extension to
an unprotected house only requires secondary
protection [provision for future subfloor extraction,
ie radon sump and extract pipe or ventilated
subfloor void] when the ground-floor area of the
extension is greater than 30 m².*

There is no requirement for protective measures to be
incorporated in an extension, or in a conservatory, with
a ground floor area of less than 30 m², where the house
is unprotected; it would be prudent, however, to
consider incorporating such measures.

The BRE Report[9] offers detailed guidance on the
construction of dwellings in radon-affected areas, and
identifies these areas. A BRE leaflet[11] gives additional
guidance on building extensions and conservatories in
radon-affected areas.

RE-TESTING FOR RADON
It is important to re-monitor the property for radon
after conversion or alteration works have been
completed. Ideally this should be done over a three-
month period using two etch-track detectors located in
the same rooms as for the original monitoring. Further
information on detectors and monitoring is available
from the National Radiological Protection Board.

LANDFILL GAS
Although very rare, there may be cases where the
building being altered is located on or adjacent to a
landfill site. In such cases additional precautions may
be needed to deal with methane. It is advisable
therefore to contact the local authority environmental
health department, before starting work, to establish
whether the property is adjacent to a landfill site. If
there is a problem, further advice can be obtained by
ringing the BRE Radon Hotline (0923 664707).

REFERENCES

1   **Department of the Environment.** *The
    householders' guide to radon.* September 1992
    (third edition). Obtainable from DOE, Room
    A518, Romney House, 43 Marsham Street,
    London, SW1P 4QU.

2   **Scivyer C R.** *Surveying dwellings with high indoor
    radon levels: a BRE guide to radon remedial
    measures in existing dwellings.* Building Research
    Establishment Report. Garston, BRE, 1993.

3   **Building Research Establishment.** Ground floors:
    replacing suspended timber with solid concrete —
    dpcs and dpms. *BRE Defect Action Sheet* DAS22.
    Garston, BRE, 1983.

4   **Pye P W.** *Sealing cracks in solid floors: a BRE
    guide to radon remedial measures in existing
    dwellings.* Building Research Establishment
    Report. Garston, BRE, 1992.

5   **Building Research Establishment.** Radon and
    buildings: 2. Minimising noise from fan-assisted
    radon sump systems. *BRE Leaflet* XL9. Garston,
    BRE, 1994.

6   **Building Research Establishment.** Radon and
    buildings: 1. Spillage of combustion products. *BRE
    Leaflet* XL8. Garston, BRE, 1994.

7   **Building Research Establishment.** *Radon sumps: a
    BRE guide to radon remedial measures in existing
    dwellings.* BRE Report. Garston, BRE, 1992.

8   **Building Research Establishment.** Chimney stacks:
    taking out of service (Design). *BRE Defect Action
    Sheet* DAS93. Garston, BRE, 1987.

9   **Building Research Establishment.** *Radon: guidance
    on protective measures for new dwellings.* BRE
    Report. Garston, BRE, 1991 (Revised 1992).

10 **Building Research Establishment.** Radon and
    buildings: 3. Protecting new extensions and
    conservatories. *BRE Leaflet* XL10. Garston, BRE,
    1994.

MORE INFORMATION
Research into radon is continuing and further Reports
in this series are planned. In the meantime further
guidance is available from:

BRE Radon Hotline. Telephone 0923 664707
BRE Bookshop, Building Research Establishment,
Garston, Watford, WD2 7JR. Telephone 0923 664444.

Advice on radon risks and monitoring is also available
from:
The Radon Survey, National Radiological Protection
Board, Chilton, Didcot, Oxfordshire, OX11 0RQ.

Learning Resources
Centre

Printed in the UK for HMSO Dd.8433880, 8/94, C10, 38938